The Symphony of Being

A Book of Poetry and Art

Black & White Editon

by Patrick J. Leach

A Book of Poetry and Art

by
Patrick J. Leach

ISBN: 978-1483984834

CreateSpace, North Charleston, SC

This book is dedicated to Rob Skinner,
a good friend and confidence builder in my life.

Acknowledgements:
Computer help Rob Skinner
Graphic design and computer layout Angela Longovia
Photos David DeWert, Linda Anglin and Patrick Leach
Editing Linda Anglin

Also by Patrick J. Leach

Meditations on the Mysteries of Life
(Color and B & W versions)

The Tangle of Meanings

Bare Trees

Paintings of Patrick J. Leach, Volume One

In This Vast Sea of Stars *(Color and B & W versions)*

Blue

The River of Life

Whirlpools of Silence

The Life and Art of C.S. Price, In Search of the One Big Thing
(with Frances Price Cook)

Kindle books are available for most titles.

Preface

This book is my gift, a product of a lifetime of experience.

It is born of love, heartbreak, dreams, disappointment, all the things that any of us go through in our lives in varying degrees.

I hope it makes your journey a little easier to appreciate (or a lot), a little wiser, more loving.

We share much in common, more than we think, living here on planet earth.

Poetry

Poetry *(continued)*

The Symphony of Being

The rhododendrons in full bloom, forty feet tall
and twice as wide
Its big red flowers, hundreds of them
A symphony of bees coming and going
The sound so alien, loud, and mysterious
Standing under this amazing plant in spring
Not one of a thousand of bees bothering me

The Symphony of Being playing spontaneously in
my soul, which melody depends on the day and my mood
Some days it is silent, some days active
and alive with beauty

**Nocturnal Symphony
Number One**

Turmoil amidst sadness
Leading to hours tolling
with creativity
The man inside
Grasping to take hold
of happiness
laughing and slipping away
Into the sea of who I
could be
Nocturnal symphony in D

The *Symphony* of *Being*

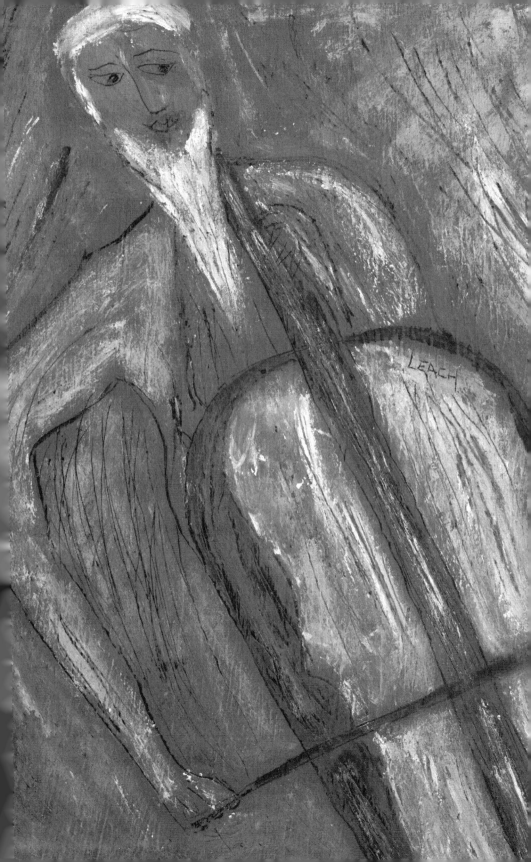

The Emptiness

There are times the emptiness
devours me from inside

Mixed with gentleness
Attempts at joy
Forgiveness for the way I am

The melancholy
I keep my secrets well

Until the hunger for consolation
Communication and love overrides
The dark and dirty secrets
I hide

Inevitable misdirection, born of silence
Their accusations and braided lies
Darkness
When even the moon cannot shine

There are cracks in the earth
Pockets of light where darkness dries
I cannot reach into mother's grave and pull
Her out long enough to tell her I love and miss her

I sacrifice, alive
                  I did not believe in death until my mother died

A Quiet Moment

I live in the white house
At the corner of the two long winding streets

Standing still outside in my yard, eighty-five degrees
The sun casting long shadows from me

To the bird bath under three large birch trees
I know so well, their white and black bark gently peeling

Big black birds looking down through the leaves
My thoughts trickle through

And lay little words where
The bird's nest used to be

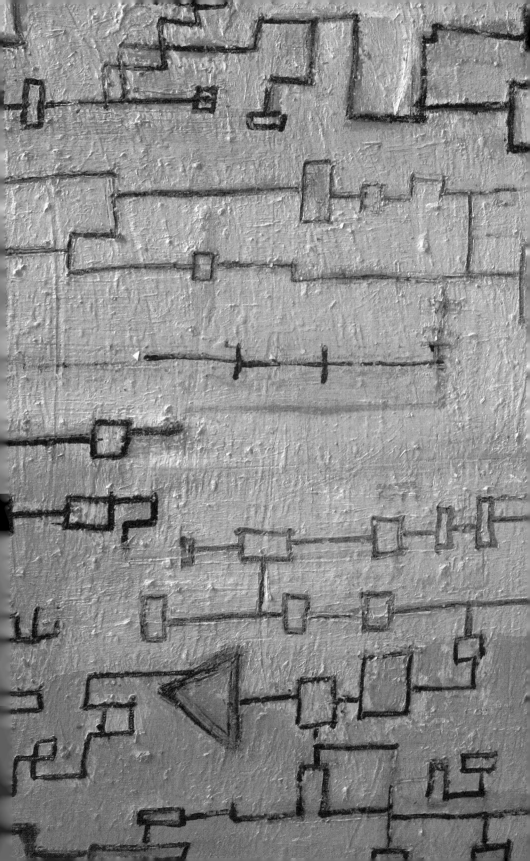

The Trilogy of Love

We approached with lilting lines
Languages unknown
Stepping stones hastily arranged over
The lonely gulf between us
The trilogy of love, commitment
Fear of the unknown

Reincarnated
Forgetting every time
Catching bits and pieces
Run together, hiding in forests, cold blood
On goose flesh shaking
Exhilaration building meanings coalescing
Seeking the Divine

Your eyes caught me first
Then your smile
Humor, self-deprecating
Honest lines
The mystery so close
Then vanishing in the light of day

Tepid waters on cool river rocks
I love you dearly
Been hurt so many times
And fear the great divide
Holding us apart
Simple calculations never will suffice

Fortune Cookies

Fortune cookies that come with Chinese meals
We smile and share the ones we like
Mine read: "Do not leave the house tonight"
It came with another unexpected message
"Beware your partner's infidelity"

"Who writes these things?" she asked after dinner
last night, with hurt feelings radiating out her
eyes

I looked away, trying to hide my feelings
My insecurities moving deep inside
"I wonder whose infidelities they sight?"
Now it was her turn to look away

We were unusually quiet on the way home
Before turning out the lights I held her
Saying "I'm sorry you got that fortune cookie
I love you and am not cheating and trust
You are not either"

She was crying, "I love you too"
As I turned out the lights, wondering,
Unable to sleep until right before first light…

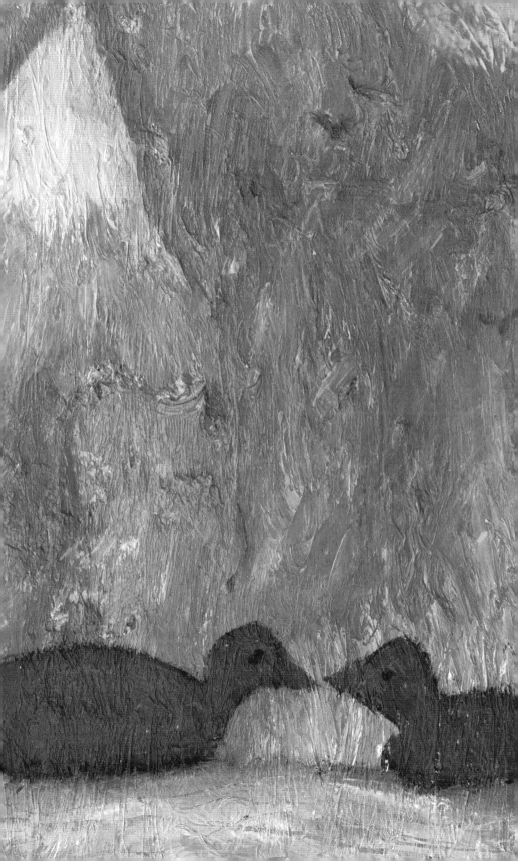

You've Only One

It is a thorny path
Large roots to trip a man
Trees arching up on top

The years go by
A blur of activity, sensuality,
Drowning out the one true voice

Inside a man
The one you know
The quiet voice inside your head

Who never shouts
Encourage, slow down, relax
Enjoy this life,
You've only one

The Trembling

Caught in an expanding universe
Hunkered down
My crooked path
Drowning in boric acid
Screaming out for help
Circling a hot star
A Divine Presence inside

Galaxies
Attracting gravity within
My being
Expanding outward
Trembling
Trying to control
Hold out
Hold in
Breaks down
The flow against it

Growing old
On young planets
Circling stars
Trembling
Trying to make peace

The Window Seat

I
Amazing how I cling to my feelings
Even when they no longer serve me well

II
So I am drawn to depression
Big hands grabbing to pull me under

III
And I would give degrees of happiness, mirth, the
Lighter things I feel for dense packed yards of wisdom
Closeness felt with God while here alive

IV
The pleasure and pain
Hot and cold
The work that I disdain to pay the bills
We countervail our moods with expressions of souls on fire
hot and bright

V
We rise above the clouds
I take the window seat
Perhaps my pleasure is yours to keep
It promulgates, necessitates
These words I pray will one day rain
Collect in other brains
And stimulate, give buckets full of joy, repose to you
And pleasure gain

Moss Grey Shadows

I am closely followed by a moss grey shadow
Moving under summer trees

Amass of thought and feeling
Walking in the rain

Surrounded by a living breathing harmony of cells
Giving up selling my time doing things I do not like

Alert, aware, drawn to
What feels important, yielding nothing

Giving all, a sigh within, not a supplication,
Seeking beauty and a universe of peace

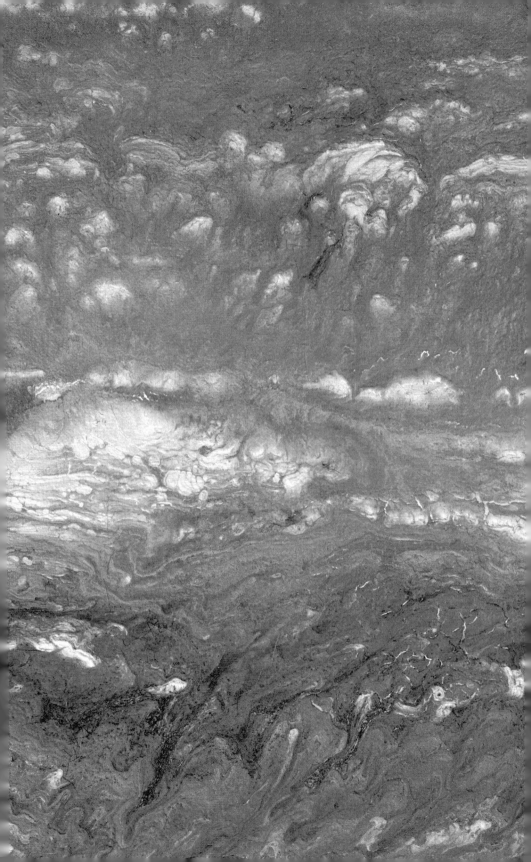

Collisions

Hacked
And stippled
Caked in mud
Buried ten feet under
Deep brown water rushing

The earth slowly cooling
Molten rock deep within
Where hollow places hide
Great volcanoes rising
Miles underneath
Soft places pushing up

The geese and robins are confused
Their electromagnetic systems
Disoriented they hang around here
All year long

Mothers and fathers looking wizened
I feel that deep sense of gravity
Holding me down where I belong
My anchor thrown in when the storms
Howl trying to pull me out
To the vastness of the sea

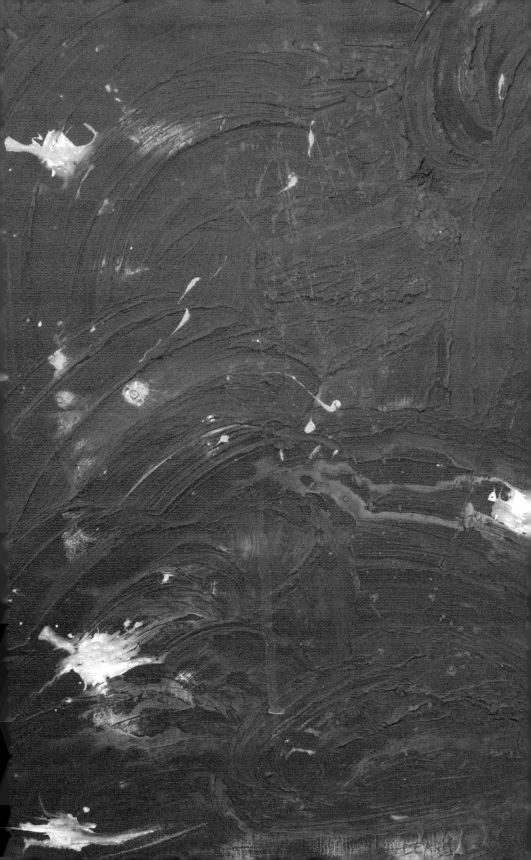

Comes
Unexpected

Out of the dredges
Comes unexpected

Joy and happiness
Sunshine through

Dark purple clouds
God kicking inside

And this love
For you

Grade
the
Up
Pulling

I run myself hard
A heavy train pulling up the grade
Clasped hands
Praying I am worthy
A good man who bears up well to pain
Carry my burdens and not complain
Give my love
With arms wide open
Offer what I have
Fight back the world when it offers me
Things I cannot take
Sing my songs
Sleep in peace
Live another day
Grateful for this life
Go willingly when it is my time to leave

The Clouds

The clouds are big ships today
Passing overhead with heavy loads of rain and snow

Content to watch them pass,
I smile here on solid ground

Healthy, grateful to see the sun
Between the clouds

The air smells clean and full of life
I breathe in lungfuls, then blow them out

Vapor trails in lukewarm air,
Rehearsing what I will say to God when I arrive

Happy to be here, knowing God hears
Despite my doubts clamoring

I saw God briefly riding on a cloud,
Half past ten, and then the little wren sang

Her song again and I thought perhaps
God speaks through birds and man

Know Thyself

As only the self can know
From within
Biased, prejudiced, this inside job
So much influenced by what is reflected back
Upon itself

The opinions of others moving inward
Into the mix
What comes out mysterious
Even to the man inside
Actors we, spinning tales

We drink too much, argue,
Practice hypocrisy
Try our best to vilify
The others we perceive
Standing in our way

Tunnel under, pray on knees, knuckles
Wiggle, wink, to gain advantage
Through whatever means
Please or surrender, be the one meant to be
Know thyself

Symmetry

Two hands
Two eyes
Two ears
Two legs
One to back the other in symmetry
Why the things that cause me
Most trouble and confusion
Are only one?
My mouth
My mind
My heart
My private part
As though someone ran out
of what we need the most
When putting us together

Nuclear
War

I grew up imagining the Russian's
Nuclear bombs would destroy us

We had frequent elementary school
Drills getting down on our hands and knees
Under our desks

Alarms blaring, bracing for attack
As though that would have done us any good
When the missiles hit

Walter Cronkite's chilling voice
Kennedy and Khrushchev preparing for war
Right off our shores

And now an older man
We still have all those bombs
So many more countries poised

To push the buttons to release
But now our children are told
They are safe

The
Hornets

The hornets take time off
Today to dance
And mate
Visit flowers
Give ground
To playing children
Stingers
Tucked away
The world
A friendly, fragrant
Colored blossom
On a perfect day

Walking Along the Oregon Beach

A huge mass of seaweed
With thick strands and ropelike tentacles

In a clump that looked like a mass of snakes
I wondered why

And I thought of men with nets
In ships upon the sea

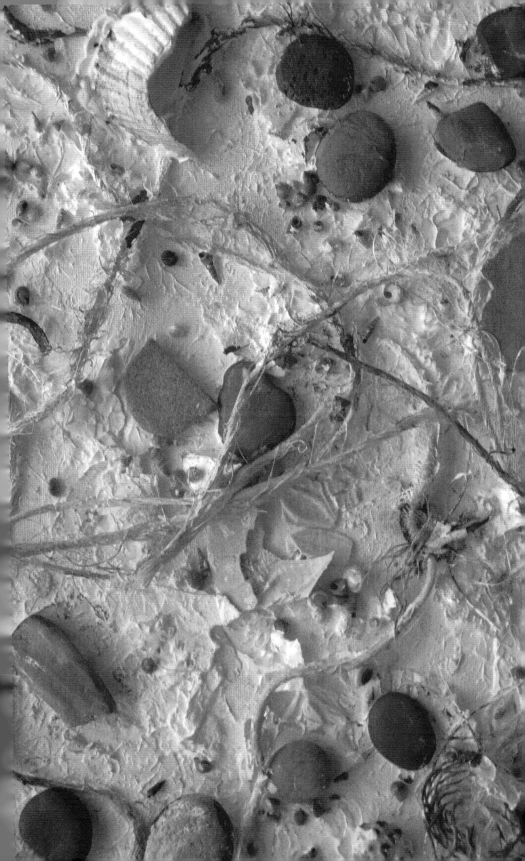

I Am the Tadpole

In the pond
Searching for the frog
I am destined to be

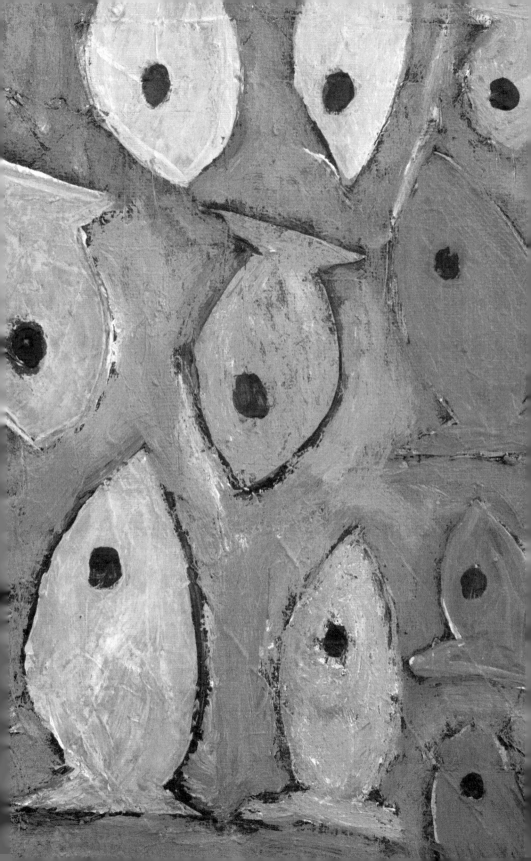

This Ever Changing

Wilderness
I call my life

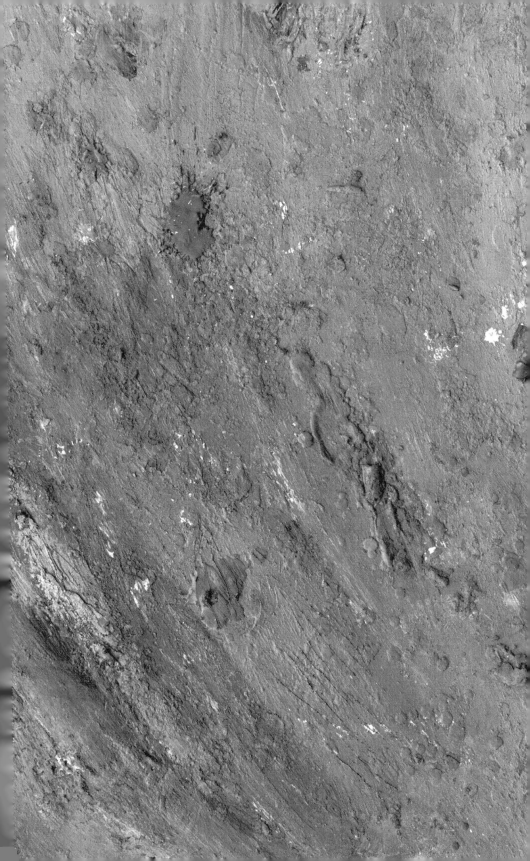

Playing My Flute

The sources of confusion
Many fold, multiplying like autumn leaves
Blowing in windswept carpets left
Outside during the storm
The forecast calls for sun and rain
Snow holding off in other terrain
The eagle lives despite our negligence
Acid leaching into deep underground aquifers
People dying over their guilt-laden wells
The insects will inherit the earth
Human artifacts buried under vegetation
Where alien cities cover the earth
Discovered, theories of what happened long ago
To the humans once like dinosaurs
I play my flute, dream of alternate realities, eagles
Multiply, it is our turn to hover over an endangered
Species list, our fate in the talons of the birds the
Aliens taught to take control, who know our history
What we're worth
I dig in the dirt, praying to the earth, fingers brown and
Red, will I get back before they decide what to do?
Easter dinner is ready to be served

LEACH

Each Man

Each man has his own time
on earth

To do as he wishes
before being laid back in the ground

In my dream
I was lost here on earth

A tiny flame on a big
blue and white world

Lost in the immensity of space
except to me

My mission here so many years,
cancelled, clouded over like a stormy

Earth with gray and purple clouds
I walked with my father between the trees

It was raining, he was crying
telling me he was wrong

The ways he lived his life
warning me to not make the same mistakes

It was darkness
that changed to light, suddenly

I felt God holding us together
healing all that hurt and sorrow

Wounds from the past buried now
the sun shone bright, the clouds

Were gone finally my life
held meanings close and clear

And I could see my purpose
here, the answer to why I exist

To enjoy, to live in peace, and work to
share the stories of my life

Mercy

Hanging clothes out to dry
In the rain
Praying for the good things
We all want
For the people
I detest the most
Mercies
It does not matter why
I just know it works

The steadfast observation
Hating other men
Meant to poison them
Poisons me

And the rain cleans the clothes
The sun comes out and dries them
It is not my task
To know why
But to do the right things
Even when it's hard

She Practices

Once or twice a day
Mozart is her favorite
She knows them all by heart
Once, she was famous
Played Carnegie Hall, Europe, Asia,
The Queen knew her by her name

Now her fingers hurt,
Her wrists and elbows
The medicine will not
Take the pain away
But she sings and plays
Humming other notes

Rows her boat out on the lake
Rides her stationary bike and watches TV
Feeds the loons and gulls
With bread and grain she does not eat
Shops once a week in the city
Walks miles by the beach

Shreds her mail, pays the bills
Whispers to God everything
She dares not speak
Believes we need to keep our private thoughts
To ourselves
And oh, how well she sleeps

Without Chemical Relief

The long ocean miles
Treading water
Swimming for shore
Intermittently
Praying for relief
Grateful to have given
Up the bottles and bar rooms
The pain and separation
But now I must survive
Without chemical relief

Echo

Big mountain walls
Echoes all around
We recollect old Greek mythology
Echo, the most beautiful nymph,
Got herself in trouble with the gods
Who took away her voice
So she now repeats
What others say

Muted Sorrows

The neighbor's gutters overflow
The rain comes down heavy since first light
Their misery stalks us, waiting in the trees
Behind the shrubs
Reddened eyes glowing
And muted sorrows bring more shame

They progressed from snorting to shooting
Their veins punctured to allow more poison
Some to bring them up, others to bring them down
It depends on the time of day
And what the dealer has
Their gutters rusted through, drapes closed night and day
When will the police come to take them away?

She sniffs the magazine paper
To catch the latest scent
Scratch-and-sniff, she swears
This is why she buys them
He drives home from work
Exhausted, and will have a hit or two
Before he goes to bed

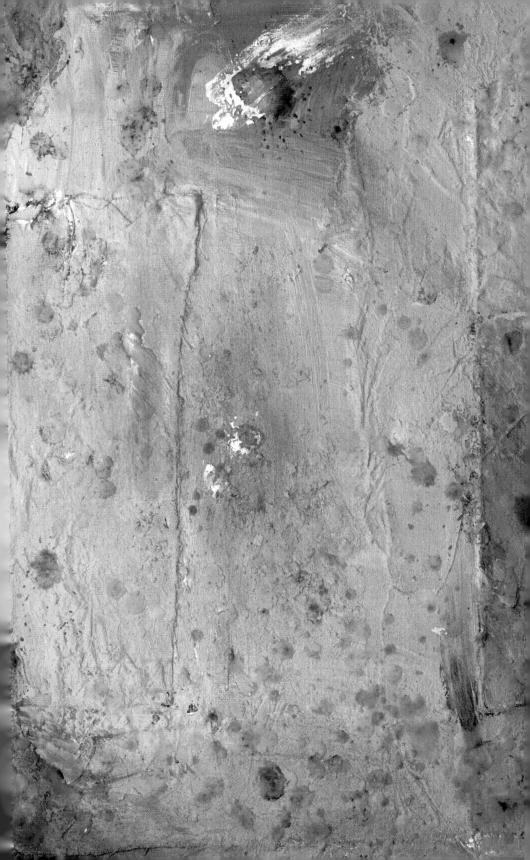

Changing Flats

There were days long ago
I drove old cars with bald tires

Changed flats with old jacks
Rusted lug nuts tough to crack free

Put on a bald spare and drove to the gas station
To repair the flat with an inner tube inside to hold the air

And on-and-on I'd drive like that
Now I drive an old car

With good rubber
Because I hate changing flats

The Affair

Short and bitter sweet
I ran from her
as I would from a burning building
A sinking ship
A ticking bomb

Easier to understand
than a woman bent
on destroying me
I did not know she was married
until it was too late

Time

Time
collapses

into lines
of poetry
like these

Fathoms
below the surface

Where waves crash

and wind blows
reflecting back
solar flareups

And I close
my eyes

to sleep

The Big Things

All day working and thinking about
The big things in my life

So much at stake
Hanging in the balance

Making plans
Foreseeing problems

Trying to be wise
And I come home to see

The robins bathing in the water
I put outside

Taking turns splashing and singing
And everything feels right

Foolish
Man

I keep expecting
happy changes
in my life

While I remain
the same

My Life Is an Eel

My life is an eel
Snaking through unknown territory
An old man on crutches
Wondering what happened to all the
Good years, a lightning strike on a
Tinder dry field of grass and weeds
A forest, hearing chainsaws in the distance
Coming closer
A florescent light bulb, flickering

An old freight train coming into
The station for the dedication
An old white-haired midwife
Delivering twins
A father reading fairy tales to
His young children, saying prayers
With them before turning out the lights
And saying goodnight

The Perpendicular

Bewitched
Transfixed
Soiled
Rubbing up against the earth
Becoming one
Stained and tattered
Achieving oneness

Let them talk
Wag their fingers
Balk at who and what I've become
An old man close to God
The planet earth, all of it

We build our vessels
With money spent on
Perpendicular horizons shrinking fast
Rubbing out the price we
Spent

I would no sooner cut off
My hand, penis, or head
Than jump off a cliff
Go along with it
A system slowly killing

Lo, when I feel this craziness
Steeping in like cold fusion
Drawing on the sun
Photosynthesis

Sandals off to feel my feet
On the long grainy beach
Late winter light stretches
Out long shadows
We walk barefoot to heal
This longing to fill the yawning
Holes inside both of us

Sweat and Shiver

The windows here sweat and shiver
It is cold outside, raining heavy stones and slivers
Warmer inside, the air thick with humid vapors,
the teapot whines and quivers

My soul purifies the sweetness out of life
I am left better, cramped, delirious for love and
kindness I cannot conjure for myself

Once so empty until you came,
home came alive, awake, and welcome

A meeting of the minds
and then you left, suddenly,
Ripped apart love that holds everything
together
Cast iron pots and pans rattling in
their places, crying of neglect

My Day Off

I

I write Poetry
Invite it in.
Conduct research into me

Seek meaning
where I divide.
Meaningless meets divine.
Intersect, phases of the moon,
this one will be blue

II

I am pink turned brown
sun drenched skin,
Green and yellow eyes on white
with black pupils dilating
big in lack of light.
This precious time on earth
alive. There is compromise
now inside of me.
It lives.

III

I respect the man who walks
his dog past my house, once
young and full of energy.
Now dragging his hind quarters,
so old, so quickly aged,
accelerated us.

This man patiently walks with
his friend. It will hurt when she
dies. We prolong our pain when
we love another being.
Our best quality.
I feel for them…

Puckered Skin

You are withered, graying,
Wrinkled like puckered skin
In the bath too long
Wheezing from too many cigarettes
Teeth long gone, poor as dirt, distain
For yourself and him

Cold, hard men come for you
Four a.m., you never sleep in bed
        Sitting wide awake
They pull you up, obscene words
        Shouted in
They demand more pain

        Steal your teeth, close the blinds
Take the books you're working on
        Threaten to come back again
To take your life if you write again

        You crawl to bed and finally sleep
Beautiful, healing, pristine sleep
        Thanking God your agony
All worth it now you know
        They fear your words more than
Other men

        They will come back someday
Hidden jewels, the books you've written
        to call them, today's the day
To publish all of them

The Crucible

When I was still in my teens
Enrolled in university
I had summer jobs
Working for construction companies
Laboring in the heat

One job we had was moving factory
Equipment from one building to another
In preparation for remodeling
They shut down the machines, we took
Them apart and moved them, tough
Work moving those heavy machines
Many still warm from constant use

I saw a man with a long handled pole
A metal pot or bucket on the end
Bare-chested, sweating in the heat
Moving molten metal gold or silver
From the machine we later moved
To a storage tank

And when he looked at me, I saw such sadness
In his eyes, like this was the last place on Earth
He wanted to be, caught in the crucible of life,
Biding his time knowing there was no better
place he could be

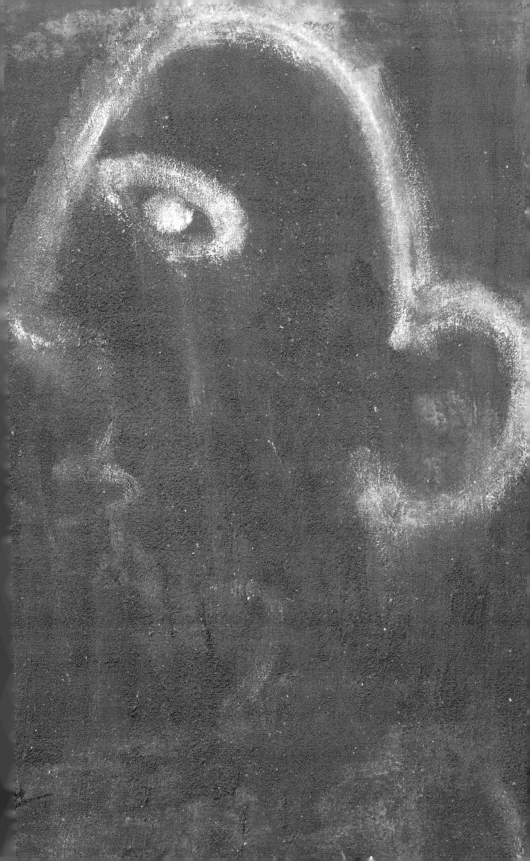

The Circadian Rhythms

Sleep walking through my life
A pencil sketch of me
Taking charge rising up from the deep well at
the core of my being
In love with someone else
Rapid eye movements with eyes wide open
Surrounded by other rhythms playing and working
with rhythms out of tune
Synchronization with the circadian rhythms of you
We sleep walk together under the sun and phases
of the moon

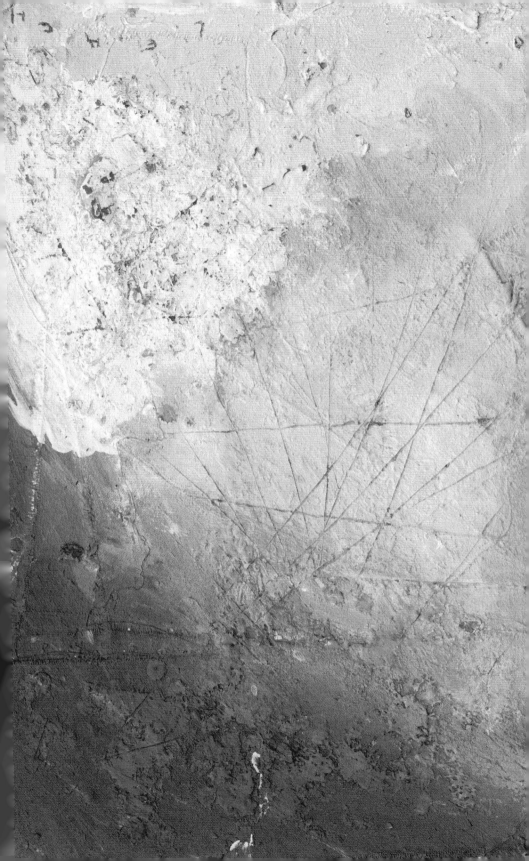

Mood Swings

I am given to mood swings
A hot blue metal tool lying in August sun
It burns when touched
I scream with pain
Seek relief in shade and medication
Mood swings in the trees
First to love, then mistrust
Coalesce in fear and lack of faith
The trees watch, afraid
The lonely man inside reaches out,
Again
Normal people difficult to find
They keep away
The terror climbs the ladder up
Afraid to jump, afraid to stay
The same
The mood swings back again,
Just in time

Prisons

I've seen so many dirty side streets
Ugly shadows crossing prisons of lonely people
Unhappiness and withered dreams
Once fresh and new, now old and aged before their time
Nervous breakdown and diagnoses rare not long ago
Addictions stealing vitality and life
Looking out a dirty bus window passing through
Another lonely city, my heart feeling unloved
Unwanted here on this cold, rainy night with nowhere to stay
I am irrelevant here and most everywhere I've been
The words unappreciated, unmoved
Locked away from people who could care
It rained long and hard today, the forecast calls for snow and
rain mixed with ice
One lonely cold winter coming right down the pike

Premeditated
Perhaps

I
I mow your lawn
Push your chair on wheels

Write your books
Keep you company

How many more days will
You live like this

I let it go
Gifts from God through me to you

II
I was startled by how easy
That first kiss was at eight years old

Seven billion of us now
And growing

More than a kiss for each of us
And no turning back

Though We Love Completely

There are thoughts in your head
I will never know

Great symphonies and plays, unexpressed
You lie beside me, in another world

And then you twitch
Revealing vast gulfs between us

Though we are in love
So much distance separates

We love and yet barely know
Each other in so many ways

Though we are remiss
If we do not try

This fascinates
Brothers, sisters, family,

Husbands, wives, children, partners,
Lifelong friends

We will never truly know the ones who love us
Completely

The Sentient Mind

Lymph nodes and nerve cells
Nourished by tiny capillaries
The work of a healthy body

To prevent blockages and deaths
Mini strokes
Working surreptitiously

To quell their deep blue sentience
Sweet memories vanquished
The mortal touch of human weakness

Slowly robbing
Its central command
Focus closing down
The steep red steps

The frailty of being
Human witness
Images
It hurts to watch

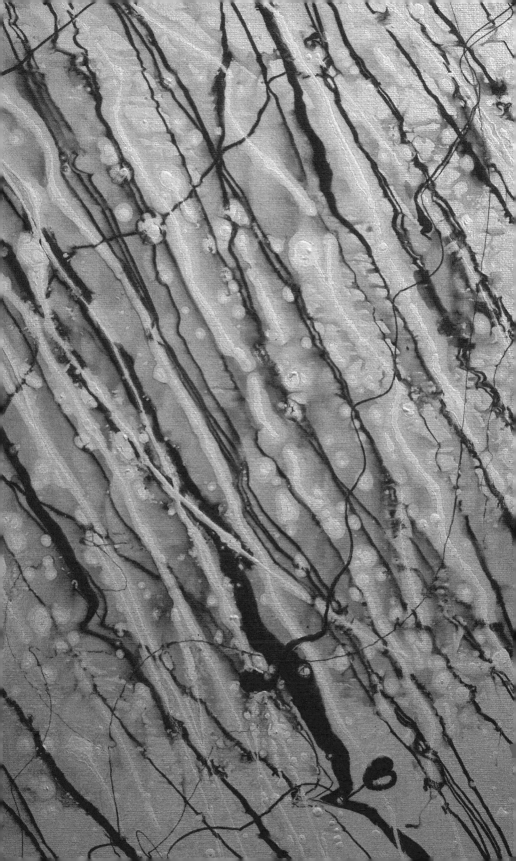

Ground Glass

The ground glass inside a man
Never goes away completely
It migrates and cuts

When I'm most alone
Cut off from reality
I look out from eyes that see the world

Spinning, tilted, unsubstantiated where
There once were friends and lovers close
Where once were rolling hills, miles of open

Range, we rode our horses and played
Together, now separated by fences of
Different designs, wood, and metal, chain link

Barbed wire, electrified
Separated, pushed into cities and roads,
Material things

The work place cruel to those like me
Abrasive frictions, the jungle, jingle, jangle
Of love gone missing

Another bleak and lonely day, sun hidden
By raspy clouds, with victims looking up imagining
Clean air untouched by human things

In Another Life

Let me be a happy mole
Tunneling my way underground

Let me sprout yellow flowers in spring
A dandelion about to seed

A blade of grass, a bee, a flower
So contented, calling to the bees

A pear tree with little white flowers
A big bear hibernating, just waking up

Oh let me be a crow, a lion, a
Little finch, a robin, a gull

Let me swim the sea, a seal
A crab, a salmon, a seahorse, an eel

So when I'm done I've lived
Oh truly lived

To share with God the many
Forms of me

Why?

I too
like other men
Terminal
Brief sojourn
Alive, it can feel
An eternity
How long, these heartfelt
moments glisten,
Morning dew, once ice,
Clouds, the sea
Why, I ask myself,
Am I compelled
to write such words
Think these thoughts
Built up like little works
of art on flat sheets and screens
Why the urge to leave
behind
For those I will never meet

The Rustle of Winter Trees

A soft scent of spring in her hair
Walking near, touching
No one left on earth, just us
The sun a yellow visitor
Between big white clouds

It was like this when we met long ago
Loving you from the first moment
Grateful you did not run away
I tell myself
We were
Meant to be
Even when we fight
This is our time together

A Place I Know

There is an emptiness I carry inside
A place I know but do not reside
It is cold and dark in summer
An open window that calls
But I dare not go
Or answer with my voice yet
It remains

Unborn children I never had
Lovers to whom I could not give enough of myself
To satisfy what they needed in their man

This and more I know of myself
I cannot give even me enough love to
Satisfy what I need inside

Tried to look away
To hide what I feel from others and from me

Cannot run or void the truth
From which I hide

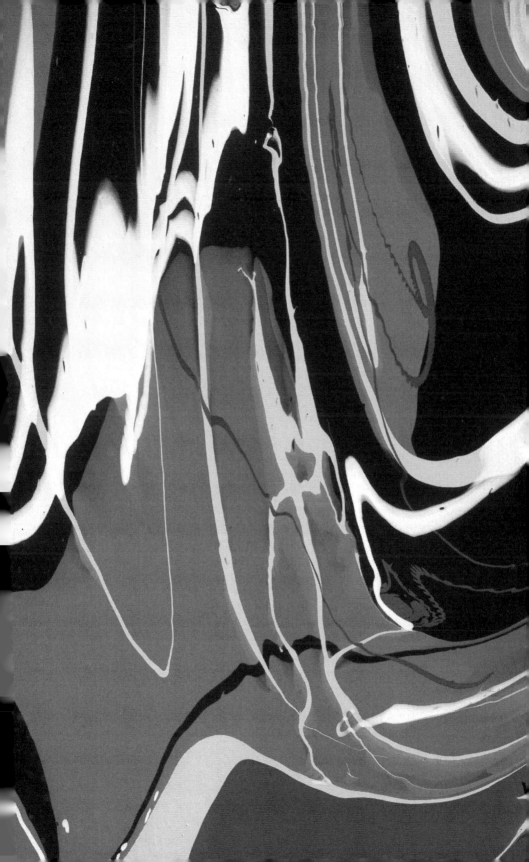

A Play that Never Ends

Love a constantly moving drama
      a play that never ends
      with me a player in every scene
            who often forgets his lines
            and says things that drive others away
                or brings them closer
                into me

To Heaven

We run out our days
Good and bad
Autonomous beings
Even when surrounded
By one another
We make our way
To heaven
Alone

The Symphony of Being
(the deliverance)

Compelling the way it plays out inside
Once born the mystery derives
Gathering momentum
In the educated mind

The value of learning goes well beyond
Money earned and influence to wield
Getting lost in library stacks
Letting the mind go where it will

The powers of discernment
Like snowflakes building up on steps
Leading up to my house
The morass plays on

The symphony of being
The myriad of experience
Like instruments playing mournful, soulful music
To tantalize the mind

Being human, an unknown journey
From distant place to distant place
Writing symphonies on flesh
The tapestries of life

Paintings

The Symphony of Being

Paintings *(continued)*

Paintings *(continued)*

Paintings *(continued)*

Paintings *(continued)*

Paintings *(continued)*

Paintings (continued)

The End for now

Please visit me at

patleachartist.com